If You're A C

IF YOU
CAT YOU
CAN...

By
Deborah Siegel

Deborah Siegel

Table of Contents

INTRODUCTION..3

Chapter I—Cats March To The Beat Of A Different Drummer 5

Chapter Two—Are Cats Really From Hell?.........8

Chapter Three—Cats Unite Through Theft And Deceit..19

Chapter Four—Cats Join The Rich And Famous 24

Chapter Five—The Bizarre Behavior Of Cats ...32

Chapter Six—Cats Who See The Supernatural 47

Chapter Seven—Cats Can Make Or Break A Relationship 54

CONCLUSION 63

INTRODUCTION

We're feline-friendly "cat people" and proud of it. We don't believe cats are distant and aloof; instead, we resonate with their independence. What people don't understand, they tend to fear—so this book will explain what "moves" a cat, besides movement itself that is. It will answer serious questions, such as: Why are cats so misunderstood? Are cats capable of sensing the paranormal and supernatural? What makes cats stare at absolutely nothing? Okay, perhaps that question isn't so serious. Shared stories of heroic cats that have saved people's lives or stood by them in death will pull at your heartstrings. It's all in a day's work for a cat.

Understanding what motivates these whiskered wonders will let you see things in a whole new perspective. Reading about the rich and famous who bequeathed millions to their cats, Presidents who shared the White House with their furry friends, and sharing the common "cat next door" tales, will help readers understand there is no shame in being a cat lover. Shout it from the rooftops. Well, that might be a bit over the top.

Discovering the connection you can have with a cat is a powerful revelation. Read about how cats protect and defend those they love, and judge and dismiss those they don't. Who knows, learning about a cat's peculiar habits might provide insight into some of your own bizarre behaviors.

Chapter I—Cats March To The Beat Of A Different Drummer

Many of us are limited by our lack of finances, personal motivation and beliefs, our relationships, and simply our inability to play nice with others. Not so with cats! If you're a cat you can break all the socially acceptable behaviors and still rule over most all other living creatures—including humans. Why is that? Some "cat people" attribute feline superiority to intelligence and physical prowess or confidence and pride. While all these things may be true, cats simply march to the beat of a different drummer. In fact, you might say they create the drums and hire humans as their own private musicians.

We cat lovers are known to cater to our cats, even at the sacrifice of our own comfort. We change our positions in chairs and beds so our cats have the lion's share of the space. We empty their half-full food dishes twice a day because kitty thinks it has gone bad and tries to bury the remains. We pick up their hair balls, sanitize their litter boxes, and excuse their paper shredding as they curl up on our ottomans and watch us do their dirty work with that familiar expression of distain. They surely must be thinking-- *How could those silly humans stoop so low*? There is definitely no secret about who' s in charge.

There has been a rash of television shows lately about cats, and they have now attained celebrity status. This could be a dangerous thing, giving that kind of recognition to the little power mongers. Of course, they rarely feel powerless, so getting an extra boost of "I'm all that" doesn't seem to make much of a difference to a cat's casual attitude of self-importance. One of the latest shows on Animal Planet that has gained a big following is called *My Cat from Hell*. It's clear to all of us who let our feline friends own us that cats don't really come from hell; they have to earn their way there.

Chapter Two—Are Cats Really From Hell?

If not from hell, where did cats originate and how did they become rulers over our domains? Stephen O'Brien of the National Cancer Institute in Frederick, Maryland conducted studies that point to a cat's origins coming from The Near Eastern wildcat that prowled the Middle Eastern countries about 70,000 to 100,000 years ago. I can only imagine how much fun O'Brien's study must have been, especially with the reputation that cats have for being about as cooperative as an ostrich in a feather factory. It can be most difficult to study a cat, especially a wild one, with its aloof attitude and nocturnal habits. However, it is widely accepted that those ancient cats are the furry felines who started the lineage that lead to today's modern city kitty.

This brings us to the question of how people convinced cats to leave their desert dwellings and enter our tents. Since there are no eye witnesses to share the cat's evolving story, we can only imagine the combined motivations of human and cat. Did humans invite the cats into their dwellings to control the rodent population? Could be, but I've never known a cat to accept an invitation without a persuasive payoff. Most likely, it was the cat's idea to come into the manmade shelter, claim the softest cover, and expect us humans to deliver the goodies. Brings a whole new meaning to fast food, don't you think?

Actually, it is much more plausible that cats stalked us as a new and easy source of food and shelter. Sure, there were still nomadic feline holdouts that preferred to catch their own tasty little morsels just for the pleasure of the hunt, but for the most part it was probably a satisfying partnership between cats and humans. Cats ruled—people served their rulers. It's nice to know there are some things that never change.

One of the most obvious changes in the evolution of cats is not in its attitude, but in its appearance. Yesterday's cats were of the leaner and meaner variety, being more in touch with their inner wildness. Today we have populated our homes with the coddled Garfield types that are willing to compromise their status for back

scratches and a fresh plate of pate'. Fat has become the new normal, with over 50 percent of our domestic cats here in the United States suffering from obesity. With no need to physically exert themselves for food or stress themselves out to survive in the wild, cats are experiencing human conditions like diabetes, arthritis, and degenerative joint disease.

Few recognize the symptoms of these diseases in cats because they instinctively hide their pain to avoid alerting the enemy they may have a weakness. As far as one can conduct a successful study of cats, there was such a study done in 2002 in which a surprising number of older cats, 90 percent in fact, had signs of degenerative joint disease. There was also proof that pointed to a full two-thirds of cats exhibiting arthritis in either their shoulders, hips, elbows, knees, ankles, or all of the above. Who knew?

Who's causing this phenomenon? For the most part, we are! When feeding cats, we humans must stop thinking in terms of cups and start thinking mouse size portions. The size of a mouse or small bird is all the meat and fat a cat needs before curling up for a much deserved nap. Cats don't need to be free fed all day. After all, in the wilderness nobody lines up countless mice for a wild cat's consumption. They don't need foods loaded in carbs, sugars, or grains either. So please, stop looking for those sweet treats all wrapped up in fancy packages. One of the things that differentiate cats from all other mammals on the planet is that they cannot taste sweets. They are missing what we call the sweet gene. Joe Brand, with the Monell Chemical Senses Center in Philadelphia, confirms this saying "They don't taste sweet the way we do. They're lucky. Cats really have bad teeth as it is."

Wow—is that ever an understatement! It doesn't take a rocket scientist to attest to this fact, just a few people showing gapping wounds from an angry cat on Facebook or You Tube will do the trick. Even if your knowledge of cats is limited, most people know that a cat's bite can result in a pretty serious infection. What they don't realize is just how serious! Since it can be a very testy task to brush a cat's teeth, cat owners tend to give up on the whole process. As a result, cats' mouths are little petri dishes, breeding grounds for a wide variety of rather robust bacteria. Princy N. Kumar, Medstar Georgetown University Hospital's guru of infectious diseases has confirmed that half of those bitten by cats suffer painful infections that can result in septic shock and bone infections and may even require a hospital visit or extensive surgery.

Truer words were never spoken. Last year I was bitten by a cat while I was foolishly trying to bath the darn thing. I only wanted to help the poor old guy. He looked to be about 100 years old, and his fur was dull and matted from neglect. So, my friend and I decided to play the good Samaritans and give him a bath. He seemed docile enough, content to let us stroke his thin body and pick him up for a loving hug.

We got everything ready—clean towels, shampoo, conditioner, nail clippers, saline solution to clean his ears, brush, comb, and soft washcloth to gently wipe his face. We first clipped his nails to prevent any deep scarring should he have other plans than to be totally soaked in a tub full of water. We were smart enough to recognize that this might be the case. Then we talked softly and lowered him into the tub. Big mistake—HUGE MISTAKE! This old man turned into a lean, mean fighting machine. He jumped like he had springs on his back legs, reaching for anything he could grab hold of with his front paws. This, of course, turned out to be me. He somehow sensed our fear as my friend and I screamed bloody murder, and then he kicked everything into high gear.

When he failed to do enough damage with his neatly trimmed front claws, he decided his teeth would suffice. Clamping down on my right index finger with a mouth full of blackened teeth worked. I promptly let go and began to put pressure on the bloody wound. We finally caught him and put him into a kennel until we could squirt him off and call it a day. Meanwhile, my finger was swelling like crazy, resembling a fire-roasted hotdog. I like to think I can handle pain, but my finger was pounding so badly by the next morning, I called the doctor in hopes of getting some relief. It took two days to get in for an appointment, and by that time nasty green puss was shooting out of the puncture. Doc gave me medicine and advised me to return in a few days if it wasn't feeling better, and she got no protests from me. Right about that time, I was willing to amputate if it didn't stop throbbing.

By Friday, the swelling had doubled and I was getting numbness in my entire hand. I went back to the doctor and she immediately sent me to the emergency room. At midnight I was having surgery to clean the wound in hopes of saving my finger. Three days and $27,000 later, I was out of the woods and ready to leave the hospital. I hate to admit it, but I was not feeling warm and fuzzy towards the old guy who decided to have me for lunch. Maybe I should have offered him food before taking him for a swim—you know, been a little more hospitable. Perhaps that would have given him a better disposition. I knew, though, that I needed to be careful about what I fed him in case the food made him sick. I was so concerned about the food making the poor cat sick that I failed to see the potential dangers of giving a stray cat a bath when in all likelihood he had never had one. Obviously, I didn't know he was hungry enough to eat my finger.

Seriously, most of us have just enough information about feline nutrition to get us in trouble. Face it—we consumers are being suckered by the pet food industry. They push us to purchase food for our cats that is loaded with carbohydrates, grains and sugars, with preservatives and artificial coloring, and a package sporting a fluffy wide-eyed cat dutifully showing its owner untold amounts of affection and appreciation. Resist the temptation. All cats require is a simple meal of meat and fat. As for the packaging, a plain cardboard box will do. You'll benefit as well from hours of cheap entertainment as kitty squeezes into the bulging leftover box or slides beneath the box's clawed bottom, determined to snag the formidable foe lurking somewhere deep inside.

Cats are not like humans, and for one I'm pleased as punch. They don't need to eat from fancy dishes at a well-set table. Paper plates are perfectly acceptable. They don't desire constant reassurance; they already know they're the cat's meow. They don't come home complaining about work all the time because we humans allow them the luxury of doing nothing and expecting the world. For them, play is everything—a happy cat's key to contentment. Unfortunately, in today's households that is where cats are most deprived. Not enough stimulation. Nothing to stalk, pounce on from above, or climb up to in order to lord it over the other household underlings. That includes the poor, unsuspecting dog. Heaven help the dog that happens to unknowingly wander across a cat's claimed battle field or territory. If this should happen, there is no stopping the enraged kitty. Flying fur reaches pandemic proportions, and it's usually not coming from sweet little kitties back. Isn't it time we end the abuse of dogs by cats. The damage most dogs experience at the paws of their cat siblings is both emotionally and physically taxing on them. Let's look at Fido's scenario. All Fido wanted to do was wrestle around on the tile floor and bump the cats butt, but Fluffy wasn't having it. Next thing you know the claws come out and the dog is running for dear life. Woops, can't fit under the sofa, even though he has seen Fluffy hide there a gazillion times. Nope—not behind the television or under the bed either. Is every place in the house a haven for cats? Where is his dog house when he so desperately needs it? What happens to Fido? He's backed against the wall, the claws come out, and Fluffy isn't fooling around anymore. That's when Fido learns that cats just don't have a sense of humor, at least not like a dog. What's worse, when mommy comes home she screams at Fido just because he may have, accidentally, tipped over the bedroom lamp in self-defense. Fido was only playing with the miserable rodent of a cat. Next, Fido's once loving mom does the unthinkable. She scoops up the little Cheshire monster, speaking to her in that sickening sweet baby voice and soothingly hugs Fluffy to make it all better. She's so relieved that she got home early to protect poor little Fluffy from her cat-aggressive dog.

Being the quick study he is, Fido tucks his tale and relinquishes his role as man's (or woman's) best friend. It seems as though Fluffy has taken over that position. He's resigned himself to the realization that IF YOU'RE A CAT YOU CAN do just about anything.

IF YOU'RE A CAT YOU CAN…

Chapter Three—Cats Unite Through Theft And Deceit

Why do you think people have given the name of "cat burglar" to talented thieves whose nightly raids are rarely discovered by even the most determined investigators? They're the bold sort of thieves who come time and time again to victimize the entire community. Homeowners wake to the realization that they've been vandalized with irreplaceable valuables taken by one with no regard for others' privacy. You know the kind of valuables we're talking about—it's that one glove gone missing, the holy hockey sock, or worn out tennis shoe that's not where it was when you went to bed the night before. Then there is one burglar suspected of a more kinky crime. He obviously has a fetish for underwear and bikini bottoms. With little hope for recovery of their items, neighbors fear what might be next.

To fight this dastardly criminal, members of the community decide to mount surveillance cameras to catch the cat burglar in the act. A few nights pass with no resolution. Next the neighbors gather to discuss whether it could be someone in their very own neighborhood who knew of their attempt to arrest and prosecute. Alas, not even the best of the best can withstand their vigilance, and everyone is amazed at what they discover in their quiet little California community. It was Dusty all along—Dusty the cat—that is, caught red "pawed" dragging his loot through the cat flap. His owners, Jim Coleman and Jean Chu had been the recipients of hundreds of Dusty's offerings throughout the years. Six hundred in total, to include ball caps, towels, bathing suits, garden gloves, underwear, sunglasses, stuffed animals, and a paltry pile of assorted sundry. Some of the stolen goods were too big and cumbersome for Dusty to carry straight through, so he was forced to drop his treasures until he had the strength to continue home. His record take for one evening was 11 different items, going for a shoe or sock and being so brave as to return for the other.

Once caught, Dusty was assigned community service. The entire neighborhood decided to hold a giant yard sale with all the items Dusty had collected, and Dusty had to be the greeter. It seems Dusty's antics served to unite the neighborhood. He became the talk of the town. In fact, Dusty is now a regular You Tube celebrity.

I once had a black and white cat named Herbie. Herbie was built like a Mac truck, with enough muscle and jaw strength to power one of those 18-wheelers as well. Herbie had very few bad habits for a cat— all except for one thing. He loved to drag dirty underwear from the bathroom hamper to the middle of the living room. We tried everything to keep Herbie out of the bathroom. We closed the door tightly,

but Herbie would jump at the doorknob
until it twisted and the door eased open.
We tried everything but putting a lock on
the hamper, and still Herbie managed to
pry open the lid, crawl inside, and sneak
out a tasty pair of dirty man shorts.
Gross, but considering it was the only
objection we had with Herbie we
tolerated this one nasty obsession.

One evening we had invited a few friends
over for dinner. We were all sitting in the
living room making shallow conversation
when Herbie came down the stairs
awkwardly lugging a pair of dirty
underwear in his mouth. When he could
no longer drag it between his legs, he
turned backwards for more leverage and
began pulling and yanking it down the
last few steps.

The conversation stopped and everybody
shifted their eyes from Herbie to my
husband. Herbie was so proud of what he
had captured; there was just no hiding his
prize. He dropped the underwear right in
the middle of the floor and then began
panting from what we thought then was
his strenuous achievement. I now realize
that Herbie's panting was probably the

reaction of trying to save the scent far up in some glands located on the roof of a cat's mouth. Through the act of panting, a cat can enhance and savor scents. Although we were so embarrassed, we learned a difficult lesson from Herbie's behaviorthat night. We had a choice to make. We were either never going to be able to change our underwear, or we would have to find a way to secure the hamper. The ladder being the best option, we put the hamper in the garage and made sure the deadbolt prevented any more surprises from the great hunter. I didn't hold it against Herbie. He was really one of my favorite cats. In fact, he was a star in my eyes, which goes to prove IF YOU'RE A CAT YOU CAN....

Chapter Four—Cats Join The Rich And Famous

Some cats have gained celebrity status. Quite the sensation, Tabatha Bundesen, owner of Grumpy Cat, made a big splash in Hollywood as she gets out of her Escalade to meet her manager, Ben Lashes. Seriously? In spite of her disgruntled expression, Grumpy Cat has made it into the big leagues. Along with her Facebook page, book, special merchandise, her publicity tours and Saturday Night Live appearance, Grumpy Cat recently broke onto the Hollywood scene. Once a Red Lobster waitress, Bundesen's earnings from Grumpy Cat have been reported to be well over $90 million. Ninety million dollars? That's enough to turn anybody into a cat lover! This Grumpy Cat fame is no lone love affair that we have with celebrity cats. Yes, Grumpy Cat has rivals. Two of the most famous are international stars Maru and Shiro. They do amazing things like attempting to climb into boxes way too small and opening and closing drawers and doors. Then there's irresistible Shiro, famous for a variety of adorable sleeping routines. It's a dirty job but somebody's got to do it. Obviously, cat lovers are easily entertained, don't you think?

With cat videos being quite the rage, Minneapolis held a festival to honor all the famous and not so famous cat videos across the country. It was a big hit, and California was soon to follow. For the past three years, thousands of friends, family, and felines gather to enjoy these cat video festivals. There's food, fun, and special entertainment—not to mention the coveted Golden Kitty Award. Heavy competition is expected from this year's top celebrities, and those discovered will surely be "whiskered" away to even greater heights of stardom. Besides reaching celebrity status, IF YOU'RE A CAT YOU CAN...

Cats have even resided in the White House. Tabby was one of the first felines to be politically minded. He was invited by Abe Lincoln to reside at the White House during the famous President's term in office. It seems old Abe was a pushover for cats, eventually rescuing three more as kittens and bringing them into the oval office as well. After Lincoln, there were more than a handful of Presidents who shared confidences with cats. In fact, Teddy Roosevelt had a polydactyl (six-toed) cat named Slippers that was fond of laying right in the middle of the hall leading into the banquet room. Many a statesman was known to have gingerly stepped over Slippers so as not to disturb his early evening siesta. Then there was Calvin Coolidge who had four little fur beasts living with the White House family: Blackie, Smokey, Tiger, and Timmy. Although Tiger was a regular ally cat variety, he was the President's favorite. I guess Tiger changed party affiliations because one night he wandered off never to be heard from again. Coolidge was so broken hearted that he made a guest appearance on a public radio station asking for help to find his beloved cat, but to no avail. Gerald Ford, Jimmy Carter, Bill Clinton, George W. Bush, and even John F. Kennedy shared government secrets with their cats. Perhaps cats are trusted so much because they walk lightly, don't gossip much, and refuse to be persuaded to do what goes against their moral fabric.

Emily Anthes, author of "Frankenstein's Cat," shared this interested little tidbit with reporters for Discovery News. In the 1960s, the CIA tried to develop a new spy program called "Operation Acoustic Kitty." The poor cat must have been absolutely devoted to its country to have a microphone implanted in its ear, a transmitter in its skull, and wired head to toe to capture top secret communications from the enemy. The plan was to teach the cat to casually curl up by the target and look as inconspicuous as possible while listening in on official business. As you can tell, this plan was riddled with problems, the least of which was making sure the equipment was working properly. Unfortunately, Acoustic Kitty never got to serve his country. He was turned into road kill before his first mission when a taxi plowed into him as he crossed the street to the park. It was a very sad moment in our country's history—sad to think our CIA would believe they could pull off such a hair brain plot. It's scary to think these are the people we trust to protect us.

We've benefited from our relationships with cats for thousands of years, and now they want to know what's in it for them. Well, IF YOU'RE A CAT YOU CAN...Inherit a fortune.

Some of the richest in the world are not even capable of spending their own money or managing their estates. Why? It seems they are cats. We all know that cats do prefer the finer things in life. They wheedle their way into our hearts and practice being perfectly adorable, all to ensure they are well cared for should the human they own pass away. Instead of believing our cute little cuddlies have manipulated us into the grave, we humans prefer to believe our extremely intelligent cats have done an excellent job preparing for their constant state of retirement. Stray kitties are the most resourceful, having learned how to prowl the richest neighborhoods, choose the largest and best kept homes, and then play pitiful at every door and window until one of the unsuspecting residents invites them in for a brief bite of food and a sleepover. The next thing you know, you're signing over the deed and naming Lola the cat as your new beneficiary.

One can understand how this tends to isolate them from the other less fortunate strays in the neighborhood, like the owner's family members who had also been counting on a sizeable inheritance. Who knew they would be one-upped by a cat? To make matters worse, many of the ones who expected a windfall of cash and property are now left to care for "king cat." Every day the hopeful family members dish out rich kitty's food, scoop up his droppings, and try to ignore his snide meows as they meet in the west wing to plan his demise.

It doesn't always turn out this way, though. One lucky nurse in Rome was long-time caregiver to an elderly woman named Maria Assunta. Both Maria and her nurse fell in love with Tommaso. Tommaso was no ordinary male; he was a four-year-old strapping stray cat who charmed the old wealthy woman into giving him her entire fortune. Maria had amassed an amazing estate which included properties in Milan and Rome, well-positioned land in Calabria, and enough money to choke a horse—but not a cat, of course. Her estimated worth was $13 million, which transformed Tammaso into one fat cat. The caregiver was also handsomely rewarded for her devotion to Tommaso, and it is reported they are both now living in an undisclosed Italian villa happily counting their cash and sardines.

A black tomcat named Tinker has also earned a position as one of the richest cats in the world. When Margaret Layne went to her mansion in the sky, Tinker took over her $800,000 home here on earth, as well as inheriting a trust to equal a whopping $226,000. Although Tinker had lost his beloved owner, the neighbors were awarded a great deal of money for his care. In exchange for the neighbors' devotion and diligence, Tinker agreed to allow them to feed and entertain him for the remainder of his life. So, if you're tempted to squirt the cat next door with the hose for digging in your garden and scratching your lawn chairs, think again. You just might be insulting your potential inheritance provider.

Then there was David Harper, a well-established gentleman who left his orange tabby, Red a tidy sum. Actually, the United Church of Canada indirectly benefited as caregivers, which enabled Red to avoid any inheritance tax or the task of acquiring a paw full of financial planners and attorneys to help him manage his funds. For the rest of his days, you might say Red was as happy as a church mouse—no pun intended.
It's easy to see why most cats haven't a worry in the world. IF YOU'RE A CAT YOU CAN...

Chapter Five—The Bizarre Behavior Of Cats

Have you ever noticed that almost every time you look at your cat it's either preparing for a nap or doing its "just waking up" stretches? You are quite the observant cat owner because that's exactly what kitty has been up to over the course of its day. Cats sleep approximately 16 hours a day, and even more as they age. In fact, the only mammals that sleep more than a cat are opossums and bats. Unlike our human children who get yelled at for being lazy when napping during a warm afternoon, our cat kids are given a pet and a pillow fluff for maximum comfort. Lazy is not in a cat's vocabulary. Instead, they look at their napping habits as a time to sooth the soul and clear the mind.

Dreaming is another thing that cats have in common with us—cats have dreams. While they may not dream of owning a Ferrari or living in beach-front property, cats do dream all the same. I suspect cats dream of an entire field of plump little mice ready to give chase at the site of ferocious feline. This dream behavior has been observed by researchers using electroencephalographs to record brain waves and pulses during deep sleep. Scientists can also attest to physical signs of dreaming cats, such as flexing paws, twitching whiskers, and chattering mouths, movements typically associated with predatory waking behaviors.

Cats can sleep in any position at any time or place, and camera enthusiasts have made thousands of dollars catching sleeping cats doing what they do best— sleep. It's often difficult to determine if your kitty is truly asleep or just catching a brief moment of shut-eye. Almost 70 percent of the time cats look as though they are sleeping, they are still somewhat alert to slight movements, soft sounds, and external stimulants. Some cats sleep sitting up, keeping their muscles rigid so they don't fall over and embarrass themselves. The sit sleep gives a cat the advantage of a quick sprint when threatened by a nosey dog or tempted by a juicy meal of lizard tails or cricket legs. After a satisfying nap, there's nothing like a thorough grooming to get rid of bed head. Restoring the fur to its original shine can require hours of careful licking and pawing, which then necessitates another hour or two of napping. However, fully rested and alert, the cat has been known to accomplish the strange and seemingly impossible. IF YOU'RE A CAT YOU CAN...perform heroic feats.

Far braver than their size or abilities would indicate, cats have been known to risk their own lives in order to save others from fires, attacks, medical emergencies, and even emotional breakdowns. One such cat is Tara. If you're a fan of You Tube, you've probably seen Tara battling a fierce dog as he attacks Tara's favorite little boy playmate. Jeremy was playing in the front yard on his tricycle, vigorously riding it up and down the driveway when out of nowhere came the neighborhood dog. Jeremy didn't have a chance and began screaming as the dog pulled him off his ride and began its vicious attack. Hearing her loved ones in serious trouble, Tara the cat went into action. Rounding the parked car at a full fun, Tara jumped with all fours at the dog's side, knocking them both over. She then pulled herself up and went for round two, howling and scratching with all her might. It was the dog's turn to be caught off guard, not knowing how to get away from Tara's enraged counterattack. Deciding retreat was the best defense, the dog took off with Tara in wild pursuit, just to assure herself the family would be safe. A hospital visit and ten stitches later, Jeremy was reunited with Tara, and the two have been inseparable ever since.

Then we see the compassion of Koshka. Staff Sgt. Jesse Knott rescued Koshka while he was stationed in Afghanistan. Koshka kept showing up at the barracks displaying obvious signs of abuse. From paint put on her fur to a gaping wound on Koshka's side, the soldier knew if he didn't step in the cat's future looked dim. Even though he lived in a "no animals allowed" zone, Jesse was determined to stand by Koshka and see to it that she had a fighting chance. Then it was Koshka's turn to be the hero. Jesse had seen so much blood, so many soldiers lose limbs, lives, or their minds that his days were darker than he could ever imagine. He slumped into a deep depression from which he felt the only way out was suicide. Just about the time Jesse thought he had nothing to live for, Koshka proved him wrong. She jumped up in his lap emitting a low rumbling kind of purr, the likes of which Jesse had not heard from her before that night. He began to pet her and was soon reminded that there was a reason for him to live—his reason was Koshka. Jesse made arrangement to bring Koshka back to the United States, promising her she would never suffer abuse again.

My own personal tale about a heroic cat happened when Chaz saved my son from what could have been a lifetime of disfigurement. I rescued Chaz from the

If You're A Cat You Can

Arizona Humane Society as a spunky kitten. My son and I had decided we would just go for a look, but you know how that goes. Who can go to the shelter and just look? So, we came home with a fluffy black and white male we called Chaz. Chaz was a charmer from the word go. As we cruised the shelter isles, we saw this tiny little paw dangling outside the door of the kennel. Brett and I walked over to see who belonged to the paw, and there was Chaz. It took us both about one millisecond to decide we just had to own this cute little fur beast, and so we filled out the paperwork and headed for home. Chaz and Brett were instant buddies. Where one was the other would be trailing close behind. Chaz was one of the most patient cats I've ever had, always happy to be included in the boys wrestling matches. If Brett was playing video games, Chaz would be hiding behind the screen in hopes that he could pounce on whatever was bouncing or blowing up on the monitor.

From a wee one, Brett had to play indoors a good bit of the time because of his severe asthma. It took him a long time to convince me to even let him have a cat. I feared it might cause an allergic reaction which would sure as shootin' trigger an asthma attack that would more often than not put him in the hospital. Obviously, Brett won the cat fight, and Chaz had a new home.

Asthma attacks almost always left Brett weak and sweaty, so he liked to turn on his stand-up fan and put it as close to his face as possible. No matter how many times I warned him to pull the fan further back, I would go into his room early in the morning to find it blowing only inches from his face. One morning about 3:00 a.m., Chaz jumped on my bed and began crying and gently biting my chin. I tried to turn over and push him off the bed, but he was relentless in his attempts to get my attention. I finally opened my eyes wide to give him that "get out" glare, and that's when I noticed him squinting his eyes and blinking repeatedly. Then he threw himself from the bed and ran to the doorway and down the hall, beckoning me with that weird cry.

At this point, I was more interested than irritated, so I got up to follow Chaz down the hall and into Brett's room. Before I

saw the imminent danger, I smelled it—
billows of smoke being emitted from the
fan. Chaz stopped at Brett's door, calling
for me to do something quick. I rushed to
unplug the fan and grabbed a glass of
water that had miraculously been left on
his dresser to pour the melting motor.
Water splattered everywhere, but Chaz
never gave up his post. He was pulling at
Brett's pajamas trying to get him to
awaken.

Only after it was over and Brett was safe
did I notice Chaz had a blistered paw.
During the uproar he must have stepped
on the hot fan and burned himself. He
was a trooper, though. He never once
chewed off the tape holding the makeshift
bandage I used to doctor his hurt paw. I
don't know, perhaps it was the juicy
chicken reward he got for warning me of
the danger that temporarily distracted
him and encouraged him to leave the
bandage alone. Or maybe it was the extra
love he got from all Brett's friends when
they saw the pitiful little guy and his
bandaged foot. Cats know the more
pathetic they act, the more likely they are
to get exactly what they want. IF YOU'RE

A CAT YOU CAN...get away with very bizarre behavior.

Let me share my "back at the ranch" story with you. So, back at the ranch one evening we had just come in from a group ride, and were sitting around a small campfire exchanging funny stories when out of the corner of my eye I spied Blackie. Blackie was a stray cat that hung around the barn chasing bugs in the stalls, sneaking into the highly piled bales of hay for a cat nap, and making love rounds to welcome us all back to the ranch after an afternoon's ride. She was the strangest little cat, so we decided to give her a strange name; hence, we named the totally white, female cat none other than Blackie.

Unlike most stray cats, Blackie was not the best at catching mice. She was a great acrobat, but all her antics never ended up with a catch. Once she trapped a mouse in the corner of the barn, and held him there for a full five minutes until he got so scared he passed out. As the mouse laid there limp as a cucumber, Blackie looked back at us as if to ask what she should do now. We all busted out laughing, which woke the sleeping mouse. We tried to reassure Blackie that we were laughing with her not at her, but she got her feelings hurt and refused to even acknowledge the frightened mouse. She did paw the paralyzed thing a few times and then simply walked away, leaving her prey to live another day.

Blackie made herself scarce around the barn for a few days, probably pouting from what she imagined was our ridicule of her. However, one evening she'd had enough alone time and decided to wander out from beneath the barn to pay us all a "I forgive you" visit. She was just approaching our circle when out of the corner of her eye she caught a quick movement. It was the mouse—the mouse that got away. Fearing that she would experience the hurt all over again, this time she was bound and determined to catch the evil rodent. Blackie made a good showing, but the mouse barely cleared a small hole carved into a 4 x 4 piece of wood jutting out from the edge of the barn. Oh, Blackie dug and sniffed, but came back empty pawed. There was no mouse to be seen.

To avoid humiliating Blackie once again, we all congratulated her on her prowess, and she marched back and forth with her back arched high in proud acceptance of our praise. That's when I glanced over at the mouse hole. Just on the other side of the hole was open desert, and there was the mouse squeezed up right beneath the hole. All Blackie would have had to do was reach over the hole, across and over the top of the 4 x 4 beam, and snag the mouse. She could smell it there, but she was so intent on the hole she never realized the mouse was totally exposed on the other side.

And, I can't forget Chrissy, our cream point Himalayan that was another bizarre acting cat. My husband really doesn't like me to talk about their affair, but truth be known, Chrissy was madly in love with him. Her wanton displays of affection were blatant; she made no secret of her professed love for him. She would flop down at his feet as he came home from work, purring loudly and kneading the air to show her pleasure at his return to her. Chrissy was a four time grand champion show cat, the perfect combination of boxy conformation, short tail, blue eyes, small pointy ears, and a coat that was so thick it was a challenge to groom her for show. The breeders we bought Chrissy from were pressing us to breed her back to one of their champion males, and I was thrilled at the prospect of having a house full of kittens. To put it mildly, Chrissy was a little less thrilled than me. When presented to the male, she spread all four paws out at the kennel door with every claw catching the door's edges. Refusing to cheat on my husband, Chrissy simply was not interested in entertaining thoughts of another man. Through our persistence, we finally got Chrissy into the kennel and left her there for a few days. Finally the breeders called us and asked us to come get her because she wasn't ready to breed with their handsome male. I had my heart set on having some baby kittens, so I wanted to try one more time. My husband was out of town on a business trip, which gave me the perfect opportunity to take Chrissy back to the breeder. Chrissy had been quite upset at being separated from my husband for over a week, and she was ready to get even. This time she welcomed the attentions of the male. In fact, she looked so satisfied when I went to pick her up I expected her to pull out a cigarette at any moment and ask for a light. A few months later we had five little fur balls that Chrissy was quick to show off to my husband.

It would be remiss of me to leave off the night another cat of mine, Miss Kitty, made my skin crawl. The house was quiet, all except for Miss Kitty's purrs, when suddenly she sat up and began starring out the open blinds. My office overlooks a rather dark park and borders an even darker street, and to see someone at this time of night would be highly unlikely. I felt a tingle of alarm crawl up my spine and rest across my tensed shoulders. I leaned my head forward to listen, but all I could hear was silence and the rapid breathing of Miss Kitty as she starred out the window with absolutely no movement except the dilation of her pupils and the slight flare of her nostrils. Needing to put an end to this endless starring, I closed the blinds and waited for Miss Kitty to vacate her perch, but still she stood—now gazing at the same spot behind the closed blinds.

If You're A Cat You Can

She must have stood there for the best part of an hour, shifting her eyes from one corner of the window to the other. This was creeping me out, and I could feel the warning hairs on the back of my neck begin to stand at attention. Okay, I will finish my work. I refused to give Miss Kitty's foolish behavior one more minute of my time. Finally, my husband came home, and it broke Miss Kitty's concentration long enough for her to greet him. She usually cried for food when he came home; but, instead she returned to her vigil at the window. "There is nothing there, Miss Kitty," I swore, but she knew better. She persisted to star and I continued to scold. It was a showdown that I wasn't going to win, so I closed my computer and went to bed, leaving Miss Kitty sitting with her back to my office door still starring out the window. The next morning I was watering the plants, and as I watered the taller plant that grew just to the left of the window I noticed something odd—a cigarette butt. Looking closer, I saw that several of the small branches on the back side of the bush had been bent and broken as if someone had been crouched there for quite some time.

Deborah Siegel

I believe Miss Kitty sensed something or someone that I didn't. It's a well-known fact that a cat's senses are much more acute than humans. I actually wonder if cats have an extra sense—a sense of the paranormal. IF YOU'RE A CAT YOU CAN…

Chapter Six—Cats Who See The Supernatural

I am a natural skeptic, unconvinced there is such a thing as the supernatural or paranormal beings. Perhaps because it's been my experience that the people who enjoy talking about such things are pretty wacked out. Let's face it, those who dress in black, wear over-sized silver crosses around their necks to ward off evil spirits, and swear they have been abducted by an alien craft are usually long on exaggeration and short on credibility. However, if there were any animals that could actually see into the paranormal realm or sense the supernatural it would be cats, don't you think? With hugely long whiskers that twitch at even the slightest breath of air and radar ears that rotate and work individually to detect the most minuet movements, cats are genetically endowed to discover another dimension.

There are many superstitious beliefs that follow the footsteps of the cat. From the ancient Egyptians to modern day America, cats have been the subject of this supernatural debate. Can cats see or sense things that we cannot? Pharaohs believed that the sun's rays were actually captured by the cat and stored overnight in its eyes to preserve light for the morning. Sailors told stories of cats predicting bad weather and causing storms to occur by magically whipping their tails. Many of today's psychics believe that the energy surrounding our bodies can be seen by cats, which may account for their senses being alerted when we are sick or excited.

There have also been reports of a cat named Oscar that can sense death. Oscar has been comforting patients in the Steere House Nursing Center for most of his 10 years. He roams the hall hesitating outside each door as if trying to determine if it's time for his visit. When the patient is just hours from death, Oscar gently jumps on the bed to curl up beside the patient as they take their last breath. Actually, his predictions are so accurate that when the cat is seen sleeping on the bed, the staff makes a call to the family, asking them to get ready for the inevitable. Skeptics say Oscar smells some kind of chemical changes in the bodies of those who are dying, but believers think that Oscar has an eye for death. His vigils have accurately predicted the death of over 100 patients. Oscar is otherwise not especially social; he is well aware of his responsibilities.

Cats have always been associated with witchcraft. Queen Elizabeth I burned dozens of black cats as a testimony that she planned to get rid of all the witches in England. Ever wonder why most black cats in New England have at least a little speckle of white on them? Back in the 1600s, in Salem, Massachusetts, there were so many black cats burned to rid America of witchcraft that cat lovers began breeding their black cats with white ones in order to protect the newly born kittens from the black cat curse. So now, we have many varieties of black and white cats. One of my favorites is the Tuxedo cat, named after the fancy style suit men wear on special occasions. Some Tuxie cats also sport white feet that many refer to as spats, like those worn back in the 1920s by the most fashionable gents. For a mixed breed, Tuxedo cats have made quite the name for themselves. The Clintons brought their Tuxedo to live with them in the White House. And, who could forget that famous Sylvester, who made a very lucrative living from stalking little Tweety Bird? Perhaps the most famous Tuxedo cat who gained international acclaim was Dr. Suess's Cat in the Hat.

I myself have a little Tuxie named Sassy, and the name fits her to a tea. With a household of animals to include a Golden Retriever and a German shepherd, Sassy rules the roost. Tuxedos were named for their black and white framed bodies, but their coats come in all different lengths. Sassy prides herself on her very long and shiny coat, which she grooms constantly to keep her looking quite smart just in case we should have unexpected guests.

If You're A Cat You Can

She's careful to include her long, white whiskers in her grooming routine, brushing them back along the sides of her cheeks like a woman would toss her hair to brush aside unwanted suitors. To complete her look, Sassy also has white on the very tips of her paws. When she parades herself in front of others who may not have given her the adoration she feels she deserves, Sassy tiptoes around with her britches swaying until people give her proper praise.

One of Sassy's favorite places to relax is atop our glass breakfast table, especially when everyone is gathered there for a meal. Although this is our regular routine, when the in-laws arrive for a week's visit, Sassy's popularity declines drastically. Sassy is reluctant to give up her morning ritual and shows her distain by not only laying on her table during breakfast but by claiming it for most of the day. Then the circus comes to town, and we have non-stop animal entertainment.

No matter how much my mother-in-law tries to keep the glass table clean, Sassy won't budge. Because my mother-in-law

is the queen of clean, she not only washes
the table top but insists on lifting the glass
top to clean the prints on the flip side.
Still Sassy won't budge, content to ride
the table as we lift and balance it on our
knees while mom crawls beneath to wipe.
This has proven to be a useless endeavor.
Just about the time every spot has been
cleaned, Sassy covers the table top with
little puddie prints from one side to the
other. Next Sassy flops and rolls like a
fish out of water to attract the attention of
our rather oversized German shepherd
named Clete. Ready to join in the fun, he
runs beneath the table to lick at Sassy's
flattened belly that he sees beneath the
glass. Since Clete has made a habit of this
behavior when Sassy is lying on the clear
glass table, I decided to look under it to
see what the attraction was for him.
Clete's view beneath the glass was
hysterical. There laid Sassy looking like
the bottom of a kitty pancake—all fur
with four little pink pads. What were
even funnier were Clete's tongue marks
on the bottom of the glass that my
mother-in-law had been trying to remove
since her arrival. Gives a whole new
meaning to spit shine, don't you think?
Since her last visit, I've felt my

relationship with my mother-in-law just might be on rather shaky ground.

This made it clear to me that IF YOU'RE A CAT YOU CAN...

Chapter Seven—Cats Can Make Or Break A Relationship

Cats are instinctively aware of those who don't really like them, even if the human tries to fake friendly feelings in order to build a relationship with the owner. Have you ever noticed how cats seem to sense one's true feelings about them? No matter how cat haters try to brush off the cat, it returns to gently paw at the person's face or circle and curl in the lap of the human in question, just to prove a point. Within a few moments, the person who claimed they liked cats is pushing the cate aside and trying to come up with a new alibi to avoid the creature altogether. That's when the old "I'm allergic" excuse comes into play. Sure, the cat hears the human's snorts and sneezes suddenly developing when the human actually sees the cat. The behavior is a familiar ploy, and kitty is even more determined that the potential romance between its owner and the visitor be immediately nipped in the bud.

If that doesn't work and the cat suspects a true relationship may be taking place, it's time to pull out the big guns. Desperate times call for desperate measures, and cats can be merciless when it comes to claiming their turf. I once had a huge orange tabby tom named Baby. Although Baby spent the better percent of his time prowling the neighborhood, he would check in at home to grab a quick bite and catch up on the news. I had just begun dating my first husband, but Baby had not met him as yet. It was only our third date, still well within the best behavior period of our courtship, when Baby arrived on the scene.

It just so happened that my date, Ken, was one of those fakers I was talking about earlier, and Baby could smell his deceit a mile away. Ken commented on how big and handsome the cat was, but Baby wasn't impressed. He immediately walked up to Ken, circled him and sprayed him up one pant leg and down the other. If you're a cat owner, you have experienced the potent smell of cat urine, especially if your cat is an unneutered outdoor male.

Even before Ken felt the warmth of Baby's discharge, it was immediately apparent that Baby took offense to Ken's presence and wanted that tom evicted from his home. Ken glared down and began swearing, but Baby stared him down. Instead of running away, Baby was planning his second wave of attack. Next the claws came out and Baby rebounded off Ken's chest, causing him to stumble into a sitting position on the sofa and now Baby had better access to the exposed flesh of his neck. Like a jungle cat, I could see Baby was coming in for the kill. I was desperate to stop the carnage. I stepped between the two toms and began screaming at Baby. Mom got the squirt

If You're A Cat You Can

bottle, and both boys were thoroughly soaked. Although it broke up the fight, tempers hadn't cooled one bit.

Our last resort was to get the broom. Baby feared the broom like a bull fears the ring. If someone accidentally left the broom sitting by Baby's food dish, he would wearily circle it and loudly hiss. You would think he had been beaten by a broom, and who knows what may have happened when Baby was out on one of his neighborhood adventures. As for us, we would never have done such a thing to Baby had he not been threatening our guest. At this point, Ken was lying on the sofa with his belly exposed like an injured wildebeest. Baby sensed his surrender, and rushed in to finish him off just as Mom came to Ken's rescue with the dreaded broom.

Judgment and quick response is key to a cat's survival. At the time I was mortified, but as it turned out I should have paid more attention to Baby's intuitive nature. Some of us just don't have the ability to judge the inner heart of a person like a cat can. Baby knew Ken was not the man for me. It only took me seven years of heartache to come to that same conclusion.

The most interesting relationships cats have made are with other animals. When kittens are raised with a different species, even if they are natural enemies, many will form bonds that are actually stronger than those of their same kind. Cats have been known to be best friends with owls, parrots, rats, dogs, horses, and even foxes.

I used to board my Palomino quarter horse, Poppins, at a barn that had a whole herd of barn cats. There were more cats in the barn than horses. Every evening when I would feed, I would include a handful of goodies for one of my horse's favorite cats. His name was Rafter, and he got his name because he would sleep astraddle the rafters above the stalls. By the time I put my horse to bed and turned out the barn lights, Rafter would already be asleep over Poppins' head. I would check in after locking everything up, and I could just make out Rafter's legs—two hanging on one side of the rafter and two on the other. As Rafter aged he suffered with arthritis in his back parts and found it difficult to climb to the top of the barn, but Poppins looked after him. Each night Poppins would lay down in his nice dry shavings and Rafter would curl up in the curve of his neck. By morning they would both be waiting for their food, ready to share another day together.

Rafter never got over liking to be up high in the barn, so we did the next best thing. We made steps so that Rafter could easily climb to the top of one of Poppins' stall polls attached to his walkout area, placing a cushy bed right on top. Rafter would catch the warm Arizona sun on a summer afternoon as Poppins and I played in the pasture and practiced our reigning. One summer afternoon as I entered the barn, Poppins wasn't hanging his head out the half stall door. I softly whistled three times, which was his cue to greet me with a snicker. Still no Poppins. I tried to keep my panic down, worried that something had happened to Poppins and nobody had discovered him yet.

Since it was a 20-stall barn and Poppins had the last stall, it was quite a walk to the end. My steps got faster and faster until I found myself breaking into a full out run. When I got to the barn, there was

Poppins standing with his nose stuck in Rafter's bed at the top of the poll. I don't know when Rafter passed, but I know he was content. There he was with his best buddy all curled up catching the last afternoon rays.

You'd think the story ended there, but not so. In a few days, there was a new kitten that showed up on the rafter above Poppins' stall. He looked exactly like Rafter, and I was sure he must have been one of Rafter's offspring. He was young and full of spit and vinegar, but Poppins didn't seem to care, and the two of them became fast friends. We called Rafter's boy Snap, because every time I snapped my fingers he'd come running. Although Snap enjoyed walking the rafters, he preferred to sleep in Poppins feeder, bundled in the warm hay Poppins would purposefully leave him.

Unlike Rafter, Snap didn't care much for canned food. He preferred a balanced diet of mice, lizards, and scorpions. Every once in a while he would hide in wait for one of the slower black birds, but his success was somewhat limited on the bird variety. One day when Poppins and I were riding in the pasture, Snap chased us far out to the north end. He was noticeably limping, so I got down and picked him up to give him a ride back to the barn. I needed to investigate his injury. The injury was minor, but the ride opened up a whole new mode of travel for Snap. From that moment on, he would cry to get in the saddle and ride with Poppins and me as we toured the ranch. Poppins and Snap remained friends for as long as we boarded at the barn, and I later heard from the owners that Snap had taken up with another Palomino when we left.

Writing about cats has reminded me why I am such a fool for them, crazy about their habits and personalities. Personalities? People who have never had cats or don't like cats think they have no personality, but you and I know better. A cat's personality is as individual and unique as they are. Did you know a cat's nose has lines on it that are similar to a person's fingerprint? Your cat's nose is unlike any other cat's nose. Did you know some cats take on the personalities of their owners? It's not uncommon to find a grumpy cat residing contentedly with its grumpy owner. You may see a curious cat paired up with a kid full of questions. Cats sense what is needed to bond and relate to us humans and pretty much adjust their behaviors to get what they want. Usually their personalities haven't been developed to please us, but rather to please themselves—not from selfishness, but because cats are survivors. They inherently do what will get them what they want when they want it. If that means pretending, then they're not opposed to putting on the dog—so to speak. So, take a look at your cat. Is it distant and quiet, or an annoying blabbermouth? Pay attention to your cat; you might just learn something about yourself in the process.

CONCLUSION

If we've peaked your interest, perhaps the cat isn't the only curious one in the crowd. It may be the "purrfect" time to go to your local shelter and adopt a new feline friend. Millions of cats are housed in shelters across the United States, looking for a family who will keep them in the style to which they could become accustomed. They ask for so little—a little Fancy Feast served on fine china, a soft perch placed on high ground for ruling over subjects, and an hour of play time each day—preferably broken into fifteen minute intervals.

Cats inspire us, confuse us, and certainly annoy us; but, most of all, they bring us great joy and never-ending entertainment. Societies have worshiped them as gods and burned them as witches, but cats have still managed to thrive. They are survivors! They have given us mere humans a glimpse into the wonderful world seen through the cat's eyes.

Refuse to join in when others brag about abusing a cat. Remember some of the amazing things you've read in this book that cats are capable of doing, and pay it forward. Give laughter and joy to another by showing them the fun of owning a feline.

Printed in Great Britain
by Amazon.co.uk, Ltd.,
Marston Gate.